MINDFUL MIRACLES

*Energy Secrets to Living
a Joyful, Abundant & Healthy Life*

DR. TAARA MALHOTRA

Worldwide Publishing by

Pendown Press

PENDOWN PRESS

An ISO 9001 & ISO 14001 Certified Co.,
Regd. Office: 2525/193, 1st Floor, Onkar Nagar-A,
Tri Nagar, Delhi-110035
Ph.: 09350849407, 09312235086
E-mail: info@pendownpress.com
Branch Office: 1A/2A, 20, Hari Sadan, Ansari Road,
Daryaganj, New Delhi-110002
Ph.: 011-45794768
Website: PendownPress.com

First Edition: 2023

ISBN: 978-93-5554-480-3

Contents

Chapter 1

My Journey of Serving People & Creating Prosperity

"The best way to find yourself is to lose yourself in the service of others"
~Mahatma Gandhi

As you hold this book in your hands, I am sure you are feeling something, excitement, anticipation, curiosity etc.; if you take a few deep breaths, hold still and focus your attention on this book, you will be able to feel its subtle vibrations. All you are feeling or experiencing- the emotions and vibrations- is all ENERGY.

As you go through this book, you will understand that everything is Energy & Vibrations. You are holding this book because your Energy and the book's Energy are aligned.

Planets have their own energies. Numbers have their own vibrations. Everything in this world represents Energy.

And it is this energetic connection and alignment that has brought me this amazing opportunity of connecting with you all through this book.

Delighted to Meet You

Namaste, I am Dr. Taara Malhotra, a Holistic Energy Healer, Spiritual Mentor and Life Coach.

I am humbled and blessed to be gifted with psychic & clairvoyant abilities. I made my first Energy prediction when I was just 5 years old.

Right from childhood, I could sense Energy, and my childhood is filled with incredible stories where I spontaneously guided people (family, friends, acquaintances and strangers included) by giving them hints about what to do or what not to do, what path to take, and advising them on what decision would be right for them.

Though I continued to be extra perceptive to Energy and kept helping people, as I grew up, I drifted toward the pursuit of regular academic education even though I felt called to dedicate my life to Energy & Energy Healing.

I am an MBA and a B.Tech by education, but finally, I chose to heed my calling of serving humanity and decided to follow my life-purpose [H1]. Since then, I have been practising the spiritual modalities of healing and guidance for over 13 years now.

I specialize in Astrology, Reiki & Angel Healing, Vastu, Lama Fera, Aura Scanning & Tarot Card Reading.

As a Spiritual & Life Coach, I use my Energy work to facilitate people's mental and emotional healing through various modalities. I conduct a lot of seminars and meditation sessions to help people live a radically fulfilling life.

The Covid pandemic has been an eye-opener for humanity as a whole; it has affected some of us more deeply than others. It has left countless people shocked, anxious and depressed.

Since the pandemic, I have been receiving endless requests to heal people from depression and anxiety, which has made their relationships, as well as life. In the last two years, I have been proactively working in the field of mental health and empowering people to take charge of their lives.

As I shared above, I have been sensing Energy and guiding/ telling people as a channeling and psyching medium for quite some time.

Even though most of my abilities and skill are gifts from nature; I have also trained formally to hone my skills and thoroughly understand the science & spirituality behind the workings of the Universe.

I am a certified practitioner in Reiki, Lama Fera, Tarot Card Reading, Numerology, Vastu, Energy Healing, Akashic Records, and Life coaching.

I am often asked by people and the media as to what are my most popular services.

You might find it hard to believe, but "Entity removals & Black Magic reversals" are the most popular services for which I get a lot of requests. Later in the book, I have talked about this in detail. Purifying and protecting your Energy with the right guidance will help people not only stay safe, the information I share will help demystify this topic and understand all this better.

Another popular service I offer to the world is Relationship Healing. We need to understand that due to the increasing rat race, materialism and screen time, our relationships have become toxic, and ego problems are making it difficult for people to heal their relationships themselves.

As a Relationship Healer, I ensure that I maintain an objective and holistic view and a very selfless and pure intent while helping people heal their relationships.

I feel happy to say that I have succeeded in healing hundreds of relationships in the last few years.

Also, I am often asked questions about my clairvoyant abilities. Clairvoyance is the ability to foresee things. You might feel that it is exceptional or highly unique but believe me, our Vedas say that all of us are born with some clairvoyant abilities.

When we are born, we are all connected to the divine. Slowly as we become influenced by the world around us, we tend to lose that connection, or it becomes weak. The problem is we do not nurture our sixth sense enough to strengthen it and use it to help people.

I feel grateful and fulfilled when I use my clairvoyance to help people or to guide them or save them from any forthcoming danger. For example, an elderly client of mine was planning a trip to Canada to meet her son. When they shared the journey plan and the dates of travel with me, I could sense some negative energy, and I told them to postpone or change the dates. They were unhappy because such an action meant an extra expense of INR 1,00,000 but owing to their trust in me, and they postponed the dates. Her husband fell severely ill during those dates, and she realized that she would not have been able to travel at all had she not postponed her travel dates.

Another example is of a 30-year-old woman client who was anxious and worried about when she would get married. I told her she would get married when she experienced a job change. True to my words, she joined a new company after 6 months of her consultation with me. She came into contact with a wonderful person in that company. Soon she got married to him and is today happily settled in her life.

Another area of my practice that people are immensely curious about is my ability to channel and be a psychic medium. This, again, is an ability and gift that allows me to help people. There are people who find it difficult to cope with the loss of their loved one. Or sometimes, they wish to seek forgiveness from the Soul of their loved one who has left this world. Such people need help to move on. I facilitate them in communicating or speaking with the lost one's Soul. I act as a medium and channel their messages with the deceased ones through automatic writing, and thus, they are able to overcome their grief.

All the practices & modalities are interlinked. As I said earlier, Planets have their own energies. Numbers have their own vibrations. Everything in this world represents Energy.

Do you know even Money has its own Energy? Similarly, Vastu is also a science of balancing Energy & vibes as per the space and elements. In a nutshell, all these modalities revolve around energies. People with abundant spirit and positive Energy attract a lot of Money, and that explains the Law of Attraction as well. Similarly, when you correct your mobile number or your signature, or even your name as per numerology and astrology, you are able to attract bounties from the Universe because you are operating at the same frequency as this Universe.

Taking the example of astrology, sometimes, we say Rahu or Ketu is malefic. This makes that person take wrong decisions. So, as an Energy Healer, I help balance out all such negative energies in people's lives. I work with Angels to download the messages of the Universe.

I offer holistic energy services to help people live a blessed and happy life. Being the founder of Divine Energy Bliss, I have been training & teaching people across the globe in all the above modalities to help them evolve spiritually and become independent by taking control of and mastering their own Energy.

I have talked about all this in detail, along with practical tips, techniques, rituals and meditations to get your Energy in sync with the Universe and attract abundance in all areas of your life.

It's been a fulfilling 15 years of the journey so far for me. Each day brings new hopes of healing people and helping them see infinite potentials to grow in life. I am grateful that I understood my life-purpose and took control of my Energy and hence my life.

I have created prosperity in every area of my life through serving people, and this book is a part of my service journey to reach even more people and help them master and control their Energy to take control of their life and create 360-degree prosperity.

Spiritually and Abundantly yours.

Dr. Taara Malhotra

Chapter 2

Who Are YOU?
You Are Divine & Powerful!

*"You are one thing only. You are a Divine Being.
An all-powerful Creator. You are a Deity in
jeans and a t-shirt, and within you dwells the
infinite wisdom of the ages and the sacred creative
force of All that is, will be and ever was"*

~Anthon St. Maarten

How many times in life have we all felt lost, disconnected, worthless and unsure of ourselves?

I am certain that all of us can relate to this situation. We have all been there one time or the other.

Yet, in most of these situations, something strong and resilient, magical and powerful, rises within us at the worst points in our lives and helps us fight every challenge and bounce back. Rising even from the ashes just like the Phoenix!

Have you ever stopped to wonder how that happens? How do you pull that magic off?

The answer is so simple that we miss it.

It is because we are born whole and divine, a powerful embodiment of the infinite & eternal energy of the Source/ Universe/Almighty/God!

Over a period of time, due to society's conditioning and their judgements and comments, we begin to lose our belief in our divinity, our power and most of all, we become so engrossed in the material world that we begin to lose our connection to the Source, the Universal Cosmic Power.

However, in times of distress or desperation, we are able to channel our connection to Source, tap into our divinity and power and become the all-powerful creator and manifester that we are.

To truly understand & believe in our power, we need to believe that we are not merely human beings; instead, we are spiritual beings having a human experience.

We do not exist in isolation; we are all interconnected; we are all unique parts of a Powerful whole-the Universe. We co-create using our energetic connection to the Universe/Source.

YOU Uniquely YOU!

You come into this life with a purpose bearing your own unique signature. A simple proof of this lies in your fingerprints; nobody else in this whole wide world with 7.9 billion people has the same fingerprints as YOU! What you can create, no one else can create because you are the Power!

Comparing yourself to anyone is not apt! Can you choose between the Sun and the Moon, the Earth and the Sky, the Air and Water? No, surely you cannot, for the world cannot exist without even one of them.

Can Fish fly or Birds swim? Yet can you say who is superior? They each have their own strengths. Similarly, each of us have our own unique talents, our own Life-Purpose, our own Life-Path and our unique soul journey that encompasses our body.

Comparisons are odious and an insult to our own power and divinity!

Decoding Spirituality!

As I shared earlier, the well-known fact that we are spiritual beings having a human experience, the question arises what is spirituality?

Much is being spoken and written about spirituality as the world today is awakening and ascending.

Spirituality is nothing but being aware of one's connection to the Source/Creator.

Spirituality is really about believing in our connection to Source and getting out of our own way to allow ourselves to be guided by a higher power, whatever we may choose to call it.

Exploring Source

Now that we have been emphasizing our connection to the Creator or Source, the next logical step would be to understand and explore what Source is?

If we were to look at the dictionary definitions of Source, this is what we would find variously:

- A place, person, or thing from which something originates or can be obtained

- One that initiates

- One that supplies information

- The place something comes from or starts at, or the cause of something.

And all these definitions make complete sense from a spirituo-practical point of view.

Working with the belief that there is a Higher Universal Power at play, the usage of the word Source makes perfect sense as

- Source is from where life comes or originates or from where life can be obtained.

- Source is the initiator of everything,

- Source is what supplies us information through divine guidance, intuition, and inspiration

- And that Source is the place from where we come, where everything starts and the cause of everything.

Everything is Within!

As I said before, we are not beings of isolation; we are connected to everything around us and to the Universe/Source through energy. Source isn't an external phenomenon; it is not outside of us. We carry Source within ourselves as wisdom, guidance, intuition, discernment, growth and more.

It is an interconnected dynamic. Source/Universal Energy is as much a part of us as we are a part of it.

The Interplay of Kriya and Karma

So, what is it that makes us human beings truly powerful compared to so many other living species on this planet? Well, the answer is simple. The one thing that sets the Human Race apart is their DISCERNMENT. Human Beings are blessed with the ability to THINK.

This thinking ability is what makes us truly special. This is what differentiates KRIYA (Random Action or Action by default) and KARMA (Conscious and Mindful Action with Intent).

This Conscious, Mindful Thought and Action with Intent is the foundation of discernment—the ability to choose between creation and destruction, positivity and negativity, right and wrong, etc.

Animals merely perform Kriya by only scavenging for food, feeding their young and taking care of their families. We as Human beings perform these actions too, but we do so much more, and whatever we do, we do with intent. Karma is the power of action with intent that we are blessed with. Discernment is the choice of how you wish to use that power.

Be a Bomb or be a Powerhouse

This power of discernment is what makes us who we are. Take the example of Uranium. It is just a radioactive material with the power to produce massive amounts of energy.

If used to energize a Power-Plant Uranium can be a life-giving source.

On the other hand, its massive energy can also be harnessed to make a Nuclear Bomb and be a mass weapon of destruction.

So is with us, we can use our power of thought and action for either positivity or negativity.

And this is where our connection to Source or Universal Energy comes in. When we are connected to Universal Energy, we tend to use our Source Power for the greater good, and when we are disconnected from it, we tend to give in to negativity and destruction.

That is why it is so important to maintain our connection to our Divinity and Source so that we can work toward complete Joy, Success and prosperity.

Ma'am may be here you can give some rituals, tips, techniques or tools to maintain connection with Source.

Chapter 3

ENERGY:

The Currency of the Universe!

Energy is the currency of the Universe. When you "pay" attention to something, you buy that experience.

~Emily Maroutian

Be Careful what you Buy!

Basically, if energy is the currency of the Universe, it means that whatever or whoever or wherever you allow your consciousness to flow and focus on, you will experience that sooner or later.

Let's illustrate this through an example: When someone or something annoys or irritates you, then what happens? You find it impossible to take your mind off it, you feed it your energy, and you keep focusing on it.

This is where the ''Law of Attraction'' comes into play- you attract what you focus on. Your every thought vibrates into the Universe and the Universe itself is vibrating so whatever frequency of thought vibration you send out, the Universe sends the same frequency back at you!

So, you must have noticed what happens in such a scenario? Well, the end result is that the person or situation reciprocates with the experience of being annoyed and annoying you even more.

And you keep wondering why? The answer is simple, you paid for and attracted that experience with your energy.

Now let's flip this scenario around!

If you can buy a negative experience with the currency of energy, then what can stop you from attracting and buying a positive and happy experience with your energy.

So, what is the message that the Universe is sending you here?

Be selective about where you allow your focus and attention to flow because it feeds not only your personal energy, but each individual's personal energy affects the collective consciousness as well.

For example Money Energy, a person who has seen and felt a lack of money at an early age carries those imprints of lack even later in life.

The Magical Building Block

What scientists have discovered is literally fantastic and unbelievable, that reality or physicality as we know it is an illusion!

That every single thing, whether alive or inanimate, is made up of energy at the most fundamental levels! We began accumulating energy, memories and vibrations from the stone age itself - right from the day we began evolving in the Universe. Every thought, every feeling is energy.

For example, sometimes when we visit someone's house, even if they are our good friend, we feel weary and drained after the visit. This means that the Auric Energy of the house is low.

Energy is the basic building block of all matter. Most people assume that energy exists only within living things. However, science and Spirituality both believe in and prove the same thing that every entity, whether living or nonliving, is made up of energy and vibrates at its own particular and unique frequency called its Aura.

Isn't it incredible to know that the bricks in your house and you yourself are composed of the same energy, only your vibrations are different? Every single being and thing around you, your pets, other animals, birds, your car, laptop, refrigerator, the plants etc., are all physical manifestations of energetic vibrations.

As every science and spirituality student knows, and now even the common person is beginning to understand, energy can neither be created nor destroyed. It exists as the basic building block of the Universe. It never dies; it only transforms and transmutes. It constantly flows and connects us all, as we have already understood in the previous chapter that we are a unique interconnected part of the collective consciousness.

The Vital Force

This energy exists inside of us as a vital force of life.

This vibration or life force is referred to by different names in different cultural, religious and social milieus. In China, it is referred to as Chi. In India, we call it Prana, which is a Sanskrit word.

Even your body is not just your gross, physical body. That is its limited physical and material manifestation. Your real body is the subtle energy body within, and this is no woo-woo or mumbo-jumbo concept. It has now been proven through scientific Aura Scanning machines and specialized photography. This energy body is woven intricately into every aspect of your physical life, and in reality, your body moves and interacts on a level of pure energy with all other beings and the Universe as a whole.

Since this vital force cannot be destroyed, from a spiritual vantage point, we are eternal souls using a physical, energy-body to gain experiences here on Earth. In other words, the body is merely the vessel used by the soul, just as a driver uses a car to journey around.

Now since we know that we and everything around us is nothing but energetic vibration, then obviously, it follows that our basic currency and our language of interaction is energy, and thus we are all interconnected.

This means that even one wrong thought or deed of yours can make the world a little more negative, while if we pool in even our baby positive steps, we can create whole waves of positive vibes and shift the balance of the world toward positivity.

And remember, we began this chapter by discussing how energy works as a boomerang phenomenon- what we send out, so we receive back.

So, as we talked about in the first chapter, the choice is always ours…..to be the bomb or to be the powerhouse.

Therefore it is our responsibility, both moral and material, to be mindful of our vibe, our vital force and always vibrate at a higher frequency.

Remember, no matter how tiny or inconsequent it may seem, every thought or action has an effect or consequence.

This Universe and its energy operate on cause and effect.

Therefore:

Always be mindful of your thoughts, for they become words.

Be careful with your words, for they translate into actions.

Monitor your actions, for they become ingrained as habits.

Nurture good energy habits, for they form your character.

Watch your character, for it shapes your destiny.

And your destiny affects humanity as a whole!

It is the inner world that dictates our outer world. We manifest what we think?

Quantum Physics has established that our thoughts are cosmic waves of powerful energy. All these cosmic energy waves that we send out help shape the world we live in. What we think and feel, we create.

Sometimes we blame others for our misfortunes, and we think it is their ill intent or evil eye that is harming us. In truth, it is our own thoughts and energy that are attracting misfortune.

We can create our own reality with our energy and buy only good experiences. We alone are responsible for our own good or bad.

If we keep our own energy clean and pure, we can vibrate higher, and when we vibrate higher, we attract all the high vibration frequencies like love, peace, harmony, prosperity, clarity, purpose and success etc.

Co-Creating Collectively

Religion, Science and Spirituality coexist. They are all overlapping subsets of the same concepts. Scientific experimental evidence suggests that we are all part of One Mind, One Energy, and a Universal Consciousness. It is the same from a spirituo-religious perspective; Religion tells us we are all particles of God's Conscious Energy, and Spirituality says we all originate from and are connected to one Source.

Advance research by quantum physicists has made them realize that there is a power greater than us — a universal power, a power of pure energy and pure consciousness.

The world as we see it today is a result of the collective human consciousness. The dire state of our current reality is directly proportional to humanity vibrating at low frequencies of greed, fear, scarcity, lack, selfishness and mindless competition.

The Covid pandemic, the Ukraine-Russia war, terrorism, hatred, famine, and global warming are not sudden phenomena.

We have created them with our collective low vibrations and negative thought energy.

But remember, what we can do, we can undo as well!

Energy is the flow of life, and when this flow is disturbed or disbalanced, it causes disease and distress.

Therefore the secret to a great life lies in harmonizing the flow of our energy and focusing our thoughts on what we wish to co-create with the Universe.

Ma'am plz give some rituals, tips, techniques or tools to keep people's energy and protect it.

Chapter 4

The ANATOMY of Energy: Science, Spirituality & the Law of Attraction

"If you want to find the secrets of the universe, think in terms of energy, frequency, and vibration."

~Nikola Tesla

The Dawn of a New Age

The world is standing on the threshold of a new era in healing and energy work.

New-age concepts like the "Law of Attraction", "Law of Manifestation" and "Thoughts become Things" are becoming the basis of living a great life. There is a new sense of awakening in humanity as a collective, and more and more people are beginning to understand that they alone are the masters of their destiny.

People are beginning to live consciously and mindfully instead of just being in the rat race materially and mindlessly. Today more and more people are realizing that they can consciously create a life of purpose that is spiritually and financially fulfilled by harnessing the power of their thoughts and shifting their energy to attract the life they want.

There has even been a massive shift in the way we view the human body. Today we do not look at it as just a biological machine. Instead, today we acknowledge it as a vast and powerful energetic network where spirit and matter intersect. A temple where the Soul resides.

As we discussed in the previous chapter, energy is the currency of the Universe, and thoughts are the form of that currency.

Our minds encode thought and then convert it into matter. That is how our thoughts become real experiences and real things. That is called manifestation or the Law of Attraction. Attracting things, people and experiences into our lives by the power of our thoughts which are nothing but energy.

The Energy Body

Similarly, our bodies too encode thought, convert it into matter and store it in our bodies as energy. This energy stored in our body can be positive such as love, happiness, gratitude etc., or it can be negative such as trauma, criticism, rejection, loneliness etc. Many new scientific researches have concluded that diseases are linked to stored past trauma in the body and our thoughts can affect the outcome of anything.

Scientists conducted an experiment where water was divided into two parts. One part of the water was sent loving and positive thoughts and was exposed to words like thank you, love, you are beautiful etc. While the other half of the water was exposed to negative thoughts and words like hate, kill, you are worthless etc.

Then both the waters were frozen. On examining their ice crystals under the microscope it was found that the water with loving thoughts had frozen into beautiful crystals while the crystal of the water that had been exposed to negative thoughts had frozen into ugly deformed crystals.

Basically, your energy system is the foundation of your health.

First, let's explore the energy system of our physical bodies.

Though no school or curriculum teaches you about your energy system, still, it is not really an indecipherable mystery. A lot has been written and said about it. It has been explained and understood thoroughly in various cultures since ancient times.

It is your energy system that holds the key to your physical and mental health, as well as your drive, motivation, resilience, radiance and adaptability in life.

Just as you have organs and organ systems in your physical body, such as the digestive, respiratory, and circulatory systems etc., there exist corresponding energy systems in your energy body. All these energy organs and systems vibrate at their own unique frequency.

However, despite their unique and varying vibrational and movement paths and patterns, they all come together in harmony to create a balanced energy system. When any one of these energy organs/systems is out of tune and not vibrating at the right frequency, it causes distress and disease in our lives.

Your energy system is based on five rhythms based on the five basic elements that make up the Universe, referred to as Pancha Tattva- Water, Fire, Wind, Earth and the Sky in Indian culture. An imbalance in the elements and their corresponding rhythms vibrational frequency also causes stress and illness.

The Energy Channels System

Just as you have veins and arteries in your physical body, there is a network of energy channels running through your energy body carrying thought energy. This energy is responsible for your physical and emotional health and your ability to connect to your magnificent potential as a divine being.

The Aura

Scientifically referred to as the biomagnetic field, your Aura is the most dynamic and powerful part of your energy system. Its functions are:

- To protect you

- To keep you connected to universal intelligence and source energy

- To carry information and guidance through all other parts of your energy system.

As we have discussed in a previous chapter, everything on earth including non-living things like your house etc. has an Aura.

The colors of your Aura, which can be scientifically photographed and mapped by Aura Scanners and other devices, depict the vibrational patterns and the state and health of your Aura and can be felt and measured by healers also. For example when we meet someone, interact with them and discern their mood, their energy travels to us and makes us feel positive or negative about them. Healers can do this at a deeper level.

When your Aura is weak, you become unprotected, and you attract misfortune and lower energy experiences as you are vibrating at a low frequency. On the other hand, when your Aura is strong, you vibrate at a higher frequency and attract all the good things in life.

There are many instances in one's life where we meet someone for the first time and connect so well. There are also multiple situations where one's usual cheerful and happy self turns into sadness for no apparent reason, falls sick frequently, or feels a perpetual state of exhaustion. This is because of the aura that we feel or pick up from another person with whom we come in touch, exchanging energies and creating a cluttered psychic debris.

Our Aura is affected by the energy that we pick up from other people as well as from the outside world that makes us feel ungrounded. The Aura is a protective energy territory that emerges from the body and creates a halo which is not physically visible but felt more as a connection. Although Aura problems can be confusing, they are definitely fixable.

Cleansing your aura will remove the dark energies that surround it, allowing positivity to flow into your life. An unclean aura will prevent you from having a fulfilling life.

Aura cleansing is a process of reshaping the aura if there is any distortion and cleansing it from negative energy to ensure lasting positive changes.

Your Aura can be strengthened by various methods such as Grounding, Meditation, Sattvik Food, Sound Therapy and Color Therapy etc.

Understanding The Chakras

A Chakra can be described as a swirling energy center in the form of a disk. While there are numerous Chakras in your energy body, there are seven main Chakras. These 7 Chakras are responsible for controlling and guiding the flow of energy and information right from deep within the core of your body to the edges of your Auric Field.

Chakras are the power stations that keep a human body healthy. The human body is even more powerful and vast beyond its physical self and it is important to understand that even though we cannot avoid contact with negative energy, there is a lot we can do to protect our energy from becoming negative.

These Chakras help you experience and interpret the world and send information back to you as wisdom based on your environment and experiences.

When all your Chakras are not in alignment, your life will be disturbed. For your energy and life to flow smoothly, it is essential that your Chakras be balanced and aligned.

There is much that can be done to bring the Chakras into alignment as a Chakra Healing Specialist, I have a very specific, powerful and effective technique I use in developing personally energized Chakra Candles to balance and heal the Chakras of the body.

Redone as per the inputs received from you also.

The Heart field

The heart is perhaps the most critical organ in your physical body. And as per science, it is also the most electrical organ. The Heartfield is measurable even several feet away from the physical body.

Just as the heart plays a critical and vital role in the physical body, similarly, it has a special place within the energy systems and impacts the energetic organization of the body hugely.

It is the hub and the conductor of the entire intricate orchestra of the physical, emotional, cognitive and spiritual aspects of who you are. Science has shown that the brain follows the rhythm of the heart, proving that the age-old saying of "Listen to your heart" is not just emotional garbage but practical scientific wisdom.

The Laws of Vibration & Attraction

In the previous chapter, we talked about how the entire Universe and everything in it is in a state of constant motion, and everything vibrates at a particular frequency.

And this, my friends, is the essence of the Law of Vibration. It is a scientific principle that states that everything is moving and nothing rests. And in this simple principle lies the secret to living a great life filled with Wealth, Love, Success and Prosperity, which I will explain in detail below.

This vibrational motion may not be invisible to our eyes, but it is a fact we live in an ocean of motion. Everything in this vibrational Universe is made up of small molecules that are constantly vibrating. Your body, your home, the trees and flowers outside in your garden, and your clothes and accessories are nothing but vibrating molecules.

Even feelings and emotions have their own vibration.

Everything vibrates at a different frequency. When you think of or focus on something, whether consciously or subconsciously, you adopt the vibration of that person, object, or emotion, and it changes the vibration frequency of your body. For example you may have noticed that when we think about certain people we begin to feel either sad or happy. This is because their vibration travels to us when we focus our thoughts on them.

This means that your vibration is responsible for the state of your health, relationships and financial situation. And to live a better life, you need to take responsibility for your vibration.

The frequency you vibrate at is also your personality. If you vibrate high, you are a happy, sunny, positive person. If you vibrate low, you will be stressed, anxious and depressed.

You will understand this better through an example; I am sure when you meet someone for the first time, You can get an idea about their personality by their energy without even getting to know them properly.

Therefore it is clear that you must be in harmony and alignment with what you want and the state you want to be in.

Simply put, you need to match the vibration of what you desire to have in your life.

The Law of Attraction

The Law of Attraction is derived from the Law of Vibration.

Though its origins go back to ancient times (even Biblical), the way we know it today, it first emerged in the 19th century as part of the New Thought movement.

It wasn't initially called the "Law of Attraction".

In 1877 a Russian occultist named Helena Blavatsky used it to describe the powerful energy between different elements of the human spirit.

Then in 1886, Prentice Mulford wrote a popular essay about it, and he called it the Law of Success.

Later in 1897, in his book, "In Tune With The Infinite," Ralph Trine wrote that:

"The law of attraction works universally on every plane of action, and we attract whatever we desire or expect. If we desire one thing and expect another, we become like houses divided against themselves, which are quickly brought to desolation. Determine resolutely to expect only what you desire, then you will attract only what you wish for".

Finally, closer to our times, in 2006, Rhonda Byrne wrote about the Law of Attraction in her bestselling book, "The Secret."

As explained above, it is only through understanding the Law of Vibration that we can get the Law of Attraction to work for us and manifest our desires.

So what is the Law of Attraction? It is what we learned about in the previous chapter when we talked about buying an experience with the vibration of your thought energy.

It is the law that states that the energy of our thoughts (positive or negative) attracts experiences of the same energy vibration to show up in our lives (or manifest). In a nutshell, it means "Like attracts like."

So you attract to you what you believe and focus on! If you believe you are in control of your life and your circumstances, you will have the courage and motivation to work on your goals and succeed.

If you think and believe the Universe and people around you support you, that is the experience you will attract. Opportunities and helpful people will walk into your life.

Or, do you believe that you are a victim of circumstances and nothing ever works out for you? Well, well, no surprises, that is the energy and experience you will attract as you will be emitting a low vibration.

The law of attraction is dependent upon how you view the world and look at life. Your thoughts and feelings are connected to your inner vibration and frequency. These thoughts affect your surroundings and are converted into matter by your mind and show up as events, people and things in your life.

However, there is something that you need to be careful about, Your subconscious mind. That is another major player in this equation of the Law of Attraction.

Your subconscious mind is the part of your mind that truly has a mind of its own and picks up subtle programming and patterns from your environment and experiences. And even if you consciously believe that you are in charge of your life, but your subconscious mind believes that it is a victim of circumstances, you will never be able to succeed in life or attract what you desire.

Will write the exercise once I receive the audio.

However, there is no cause for worry, as in this book, I will be sharing with you the tools, techniques and hacks to shift the paradigm of your subconscious mind to what you want it to believe and think.

Isn't Gravity Real? Well, so is the Law of Attraction!

A lot of people dismiss the Laws of Vibration and Attraction. However, they are as real and as scientific as the Law of Gravity.

Can you see, touch or hear gravity? No, of course not, but you can experience it repeatedly, impartially without fail. Whenever you drop an object, it never flies or moves upwards. It always falls to the ground, and you believe in gravity.

That is exactly how the Law of Attraction and Vibration work. You might not be able to see, hear or touch it or even be able to explain why it works. But, you can observe and experience what it does.

And yes, it is as real as gravity!

Chapter 5

You are BLOCKED; because Your Energy is BLOCKED

"An entire sea of water can't sink a ship unless it gets inside the ship. Similarly, the negativity of the world can't put you down unless you allow it to get inside you."

~Goi Nasu

Most of the time, we all have aspects of our lives that are flowing and effortless, and everything seems to be going right, and then there are parts of our life where we just can't seem to move forward no matter how hard we try.

Some of you may have health issues, some may be having trouble with your relationships, others may be struggling financially, and some of you could be worried about success in your career or business.

And believe me, I understand that many of you could be in a situation where you are stuck in every area of your life, and nothing seems to be working at all. Numerous clients come to me in such a situation, and I help them turn their life around 360 degrees.

The reason you are blocked and stuck is that your energy is blocked.

For our energy, our vital life force to flow freely through our body and mind, and for our vibrations to be in rhythm, it is essential that our Chakras, especially the primary 7 Chakras, should be open and in a state of balance and alignment.

The moment any of these Chakras, the energy centers get blocked, it hampers the free and balanced flow of energy.

This leads to stagnation of energy which can result in physical, emotional, financial and spiritual distress or ailments because energy is meant to be flowing and in motion always.

When any of the energy centers is blocked, the corresponding areas begin to vibrate at a lower frequency, thus attracting lower experiences in the related areas.

However, most of us begin to blame other people or circumstances for these low and frustrating situations instead of realizing that it is our own blocked, low energy that is causing these stressful situations.

Below, let's take a look at the Chakras and how blocked energy can affect your life through your Chakras.

1. The Root Chakra (Muladhara)

The root Chakra is the first of the 7 main Chakras and sits at the base of your spine, almost at the inner part of your tailbone.

As the name suggests, it is associated with the base or foundation of your life. It is responsible for keeping you grounded and helps you withstand and overcome challenges. This is the Chakra whose energy makes you feel a sense of security and stability.

It is the first piece of the energy jigsaw puzzle that keeps your life in flow, bliss and prosperity.

When this Chakra is in a state of balance, you'll feel supported, connected, grounded, and safe.

However, when the energy in this Chakra is blocked, you will have:

- Health concerns in your immune system, tail bone, rectum, legs and feet.

- Concerns regarding the male reproductive organs and the prostate gland.

- You will also be prone to knee pain, arthritis, sciatica, eating disorders, and constipation.

- You will struggle with and be stressed about money and financial security.

2. The Sacral Chakra (Swadhishthana)

This Chakra is positioned below the navel.

This Sacral Chakra is associated with creative and sexual energy. The energy of this Chakra is what enables you to connect to emotions, both your own and those of others. When this Chakra is balanced, you'll be empowered to express your authentic creativity and even take creative risks. The free-flowing and balanced energy of this Chakra allows and empowers you to embrace your sexuality, and also be connected to others easily and be outgoing.

- Imbalances in the energy flow of this Chakra can manifest as:

- Concerns with sexual and reproductive health.

- Kidney & urinary problems.

- Pain in the lower back, hip and pelvis.

- Your inability to express or display your emotions.

- Unfulfilled sexual life.

- Inability to handle relationships due to a fear of being betrayed.

3. The Solar Plexus Chakra (Manipura)

This Chakra is positioned in your abdomen, and this is the Chakra that gives you confidence and is responsible for your self-esteem. When this Chakra is balanced, it helps you feel in complete control of your life, and you'll be filled with self-respect and self-compassion.

When this Chakra is out of balance, you will:

- Struggle with digestive issues.

- Suffer from chronic fatigue and the desire to do nothing.

- Also often have pancreatic and gallbladder concerns.

- Be highly critical of yourself and feel unworthy and undeserving.

- Be besieged by a fear of rejection constantly.

4. The Heart Chakra (Anahata)

This Chakra, as is evident from the name, is located in the heart region, almost in the center of your chest, close to the heart. And, of course, no surprises here; this Chakra is associated with our ability to love and have compassion.

When this Chakra's energy is in balance, it will fill you up with love, compassion, gratitude and joy for everyone around you. It will also make it easy for you to forgive others.

However, when blocked, this Chakra will cause:

- Asthma and breathing issues.

- Concerns with the shoulders and upper back.

- Arm and wrist pain.

- You are to be over-loving and over-possessive resulting in suffocation, jealousy, and bitterness in the relationship.

- Constant fear and anxiety of being alone in your life.

5. The Throat Chakra (Vishuddha)

This Chakra is located in your throat. It is associated with your ability to communicate verbally. When the energy of this Chakra is balanced, you'll be honest and truthful in a firm yet unaggressive manner and will be able to articulate your point of view easily and respectfully.

- However, when this Chakra is out of balance, you will have:

- Thyroid issues.

- A sore throat.

- Ear infections.

- Neck and shoulder pain.

- Issues in expressing yourself honestly and speaking your truth.

- Constant fear of not being in control.

6. The Third-Eye Chakra (Ajna)

It is located right in the middle of the eyebrows, in the center of your forehead. When its energy is in balance, you'll be very focused and determined on your goals and actions, yet you will be flexible and open to receiving advice and guidance from others.

When this Chakra is out of balance, you will have:

- Headaches.

- Blurred vision and eye strain.

- Sinus issues.

- Moodiness and stubbornness.

- A lack of clarity on your goals and purpose, and career.

7. The Crown Chakra (Sahasrara)

It is located right at the top of the head, almost in the centre. When the energy of this Chakra is in balance, you will be connected firmly to Universal Intelligence and have an unshakeable trust in your inner guidance. This will lead to you taking the right decisions in alignment with your life purpose leading to success, prosperity and fulfillment.

But when the crown Chakra is blocked, you will have:

- Rigid thoughts.

- Analysis paralysis.

- A constant fear of alienation.

- Doubt, procrastination and indecisiveness.

And remember, it is not only possible but likely that your energy could have energy imbalances and blockages in more than one Chakra.

This happens because when one Chakra gets blocked, the other Chakras either begin to compensate for it and become overactive or will follow the lead of the other Chakra and become underactive.

Now that you understand how your blocked energy can affect your life negatively and send it haywire, it is necessary to look into the primary reasons that can lead to and cause these energy blockages. So, let's explore them one by one.

Suppressing Your Emotions and Trauma

Right from your childhood, you go through so many experiences in your life, and you respond to these experiences with emotions. Some of these emotions may be pleasant, and others may not. However, you may not always express these negative emotions. Also, some of these experiences may even be traumatic for you.

It is not easy to process and deal with negative, painful emotions head-on and most people often find it easier just to ignore/suppress those emotions rather than voicing them or dealing with them, which could give rise to conflict.

And, thus suppressing emotions and trauma is the most common reason for energy blocks.

However, it is crucial to identify, acknowledge, express and release our negative emotions. As it impacts your health and well being in every way: physically, mentally, financially and spiritually.

If you don't acknowledge and process the pain, it will keep resurfacing, or it could turn inwards as anger, fear, shame, guilt, unworthiness or anxiety toward yourself. Your body will trap the trauma energy and turn it into matter which will block the free flow of your energy. Eventually, this will manifest in physical symptoms such as digestive issues, insomnia, fatigue, anxiety, depression etc.

Or the suppressed emotions could be stored in your mind as a limiting belief. For example, if you saw your parents struggling with money and didn't understand or question the reasons behind this lack. You could build the belief at an early age that money is difficult to come by or make. This belief could damage you for the rest of your life, never allowing you to have money no matter how talented or hard working you may be.

Similarly, if you saw your parent's divorce in an ugly manner as a child, you might have suppressed your trauma and resentment and gone ahead to live a normal life with both of them individually.

But later in life, this could manifest as a block in your relationships subconsciously at the energy level.

Denying Your True Self and Calling

So many times, you go through the motions of life on auto-pilot as per the expectations of society and family. Go to college, acquire a degree that can provide a stable income, get married, have kids, and all the milestones are accomplished. On the face of it, you have everything going for you. Yet you feel a sense of unease, and you feel unfulfilled. And then you wonder, "Am I g]oing crazy?" "Why am I not happy?" or you might wonder, "How did I get here?"

But then something else takes up your attention, and these thoughts are ignored and buried as quickly as they had come.

When you ignore yourself and your true intentions and your true calling, you give up on what you value most. If you really want to know who you truly are at your core and what your purpose is, you must first listen to your inner voice.

That voice is your intuition, your "gut feeling", and your guide that comes from your connection to universal intelligence.

When your energy is stuck in denial, avoidance or fear and you're disconnected from your deepest desires, your inner voice becomes muffled and difficult to hear. And this is another common reason for blocked energy.

Not owning and expressing who you are and following a path just for money will never give you the life you want and dream of.

Prioritizing Your Needs Last

This reason is true for all genders, but it is more so for women.

So, you have a million things crowding your attention. The house needs cleaning, the baby needs to be fed, that work meeting needs planning, the older kids need assistance with their homework, the parents need a doctor's visit, and the dog needs grooming.

But where do your needs fit in? You often give away more energy to others and their needs than to your own.

Majorly this happens because in most cultures, and especially in Indian culture, we are always taught that it is selfish to focus on ourselves. This is a huge myth! Compassion for others is easy, but compassion for the self is a difficult task.

But let me illustrate this with a very simple example and often used phrase, "You can only give from a full cup." If you have very little tea in your cup and a friend walks in, you can't offer to share it with them because there just isn't enough. However, if you had a full cup of tea, you could have shared half with them.

So, if you don't pay attention to your needs and energy, you will be operating from an empty cup and will block your own energy trying to manage everything around you. When your energy is blocked, you are doing no good to yourself or those around you.

So, put on your own oxygen mask first, clear and maintain your energy before spreading it out thin and blocking yourself.

Allowing Other People's Toxic Energy to Overpower Your Own

I'm sure at one time or the other, you've walked into a space and felt the tension in the air or instantly felt low or uncomfortable. Sometimes you might have felt the hair on your neck rising. All these are signs that you've experienced negative energy from other people.

And most of you don't know how to protect your energy. When you don't know how to protect yourself from other's energy, you take it on like it's your own.

And, you begin to feel exactly like the negative energy you've absorbed, but most of you may not even realize what is happening.

To avoid taking on others' energy, creating and maintaining protective boundaries is essential. When your boundaries are weak, unprotected, or unclear, you let in all sorts of energy and emotions that aren't actually yours. And, you unconsciously give away your own personal energy to others, leaving you feeling drained or overwhelmed. Taking on other's toxic energy is also a common reason for energy and life blockage.

Therefore, to live a healthy, wealthy and successful life filled with love, it is essential that your energy and beliefs should not be blocked.

In the later chapters, I will be discussing how to keep your energy in flow and overcome blocks to manifest love, money, success and relationships etc. individually.

Chapter 6

BLACK MAGIC: The Blame Game

*"Take charge of your own energy. Don't
blame anyone else. You control you."*

~ Anonymous

Is Black Magic Real?

Often in life, people come to me in dire straits where nothing
in life seems to be working for them despite all their best
efforts. Health, wealth, relationships and career all seem to be
at an all-time low. They have tried numerous Healing

Modalities, Pooja-Paath, Healers, Pundits and all Spiritual Mentors, yet they are bereft of all hope and faith.

At such times we are faced with the big question:

Is this Black Magic???

And then comes the even more critical question:

Does Black Magic even exist???

Then there are more related questions:

Is there really an Evil Eye???

People often talk about Nazar:

Is Nazar Lag Gayi a real concept???

Wherever I go, and whenever I am interviewed, I am always asked these questions:

Do all these things exist, and if they do, is there any cure for Black Magic or Evil Eye?

As an Occult Science and Psychic Energy specialist, here is my answer to everyone and especially to people who are facing odd and negative things in their life without any fault of theirs:

Yes, they all exist!!!

However, before you get alarmed or disheartened, please know that Black magic can be cured and reversed.

Also, we can take measures to safeguard ourselves from Black Magic or the Evil Eye so that we remain protected; after all, as the wise say, prevention is always better than cure.

But before diving in any further, we first need to understand what Black Magic is?

"Black magic is directing negative forces and energy toward someone's life to destroy their happiness. It is deliberately or intentionally done with malice by an outsider or even by someone within the family to make your life miserable.

But as I already clarified earlier, the good news is that Black Magic can be cured and reversed.

In today's materialistic and intensely competitive world, people are more focused on what others are doing and achieving rather than working sincerely toward their own wellbeing while wishing well for those around them.

Unfortunately, the world today is infested with ill-minded people who are extremely jealous of others' popularity and prosperity. The desire to outdo others is so intense that in order to block others' prosperity and destroy others' lives, they use all ways and means to achieve the same.

It All Boils Down to Energy

There is no cause for worry, however. It is my firm belief in the wisdom of our Scriptures, Vedas and Dharma… that Karma is very powerful. People who do wrong to others will receive the same back through the "Law of Reciprocity". Sadly, people don't understand the same and indulge in witchcraft or black magic.

So, now the question arises how does one know someone is under the effect of Black Magic? How do you notice Black Magic? What are the signs to look out for?

Cinema and media have dramatized Black Magic to the extreme. The signs are not like what you see in movies. Let me tell you that the signs look nothing like finding dead animals in the home or seeing blood spots on the victim's hair or clothes or cracks in pictures etc...... These are all just dramatic effects.

Real Black Magic can be noticed and identified when the situations in your life deteriorate beyond your hope or control.

I firmly believe that we are always divinely protected, and even in hopeless situations, God or the Universe supports us. Still, if things continue to go wrong one after another, even when you are trying to do your best... that definitely means there is some negative energy at work in your life.

For example, if there are constant arguments in the family and a feeling of dysfunctionality has crept in without anyone actually doing anything wrong, it's a reflection of black magic.

Similarly, if someone in your family keeps falling sick regularly or continuously or if they are losing sleep or having dark thoughts or nightmares and getting hallucinations, this is also a sign of Black Magic.

But as I have been saying right from the beginning of this book, it all boils down to your energy; Black Magic and its associated energies work at a very low level. "Blockages in Aura or Chakras create various issues in our daily life or can even attract black magic and psychic attacks. Cleansing your aura will remove the dark energies that surround it, allowing positivity to flow into your life. An unclean aura will prevent you from having a fulfilling life [In an earlier chapter I have already discussed and explained about Aura Cleansing].So purify yourself first. Uplift your energy and vibration to rise above the negative vibration of the dark energy.

Your energy upliftment is the first and most critical step, so rather than focusing on who has done what and blaming those who have ill intentions toward you. Focus on uplifting your energy because only then will any rituals and remedies work. Purify yourself first.

Now your next logical question, I am sure, is: How do I purify my energy?

Purify your Aura and neural energy by doing pranayama, fasting and detoxing for at least a day, eating very Satvik food, and avoiding alcohol and meat. If you practice this for even a week, then your energy field gets purified significantly, and you will start vibrating higher.

As I have said earlier also, it is my firm belief that the Universe always supports good intentions, so if you have noticed or suspect Black Magic or Evil Eye in your home or in your life or in your loved one's life, you should continue doing good deeds. Walk firm on the path of truth and goodness and follow some rituals that I will share with you to reverse the effect of Black Magic.

Safeguard & Protect Yourself from Black Magic

I assure you that it is possible to eliminate the effect of Black Magic, Evil Eye, Jinxes, Psychic Attacks, Bad Spirits or any Sorcery done on a person.

It is completely possible to safeguard your family and protect them from any or all kinds of Black Magic.

A good, intuitive, trained and experienced energy healer will be able to guide you with remedies and rituals that are permanent and give you long-term results.

I have personally healed and reversed innumerable clients who were under the clutches of Black Magic.

Add a case study/testimonial here

Let me share with you some easy-to-follow yet extremely powerful recommendations and rituals to reverse and cure Black Magic –

- Apart from purifying your energy and doing good deeds, first of all, seek a trustworthy healer/occult science specialist who truly knows what they are doing,

- Then do the Poojas and rituals as recommended or guided by them.

- As long as the effect of pooja is there, you will stay safe, later, it is possible the negative energy may come back with propelled force.

- Therefore raising your energy and vibration is important for sustainable, long-lasting results. The surest way to safeguard yourself is to lift up your vibrational frequency through healing modalities such as Chakra Balancing, Aura Healing & Cleansing, Crystal Healing etc.

- The next step is to please your family deity. Everyone has an ancestral family deity whom they worship and look up to. Feed the poor and hungry with a Prayer to your family deity to protect your family. Do that at least once in six months.

- The final step is to involve yourself in some powerful Prayer that uplifts you and makes you potent enough to fight such evil influences. A prayer that can strengthen your willpower and shield your Aura from vibrational influences. However, to have the best effects, the prayer needs to be done in the early hours of dawn in your pooja room after taking a bath.

- The best and most powerful prayer on Earth is to chant the Gayatri mantra 108 times daily. With the power of this Mantra as a shield, no force on this planet can harm you and your family, rest assured.

- Though no two cases are ever the same, yet doing all this for 40 days will make a big difference to your lives.

Chapter 7

UNBLOCK YOUR WEALTH: Sure-fire Secrets To Manifesting MONEY

"Money at its very essence is energy, and all energy can be attracted or repelled."
~Andrea Bolder

Wealth & Money are Energy

By now, all of you are aware that you can attract and manifest anything so long as your energy is free-flowing and unblocked.

The same goes for wealth and money specifically.

It is all energy, and the bottom line is that either you are repelling that energy or you are attracting that energy.

You might have noticed that some people naturally attract wealth and money with minimal effort and struggle, while others do not get the same prosperous results with even more effort.

So what is it that differentiates these people?

It is their energetic relationship with money that makes the crucial difference. If your energetic relationship with money is positive and healthy, you will attract money effortlessly. Whereas if your energetic relationship with money is blocked and negative, you will keep repelling it no matter what you do.

I will give you an example of a client who came to me because he never had a great relationship with money despite having a significant bank balance and owning a good home and an expensive car. He always felt uneasy with money, like he needed to earn more and would never have sufficient.

When i began working with him I realized that there was no money issue in his astrological chart or in his numerological calculations. Nor wash is personal money energy off or misaligned and yet here he was, troubled about money.

So as is my practice, i decided to dig deep and found that his relationship with money was unsettled as he carried childhood traum about money in his energy system.

His father was an extremely miserly person and withheld even the basics of life from them. Their material needs were fulfilled with great difficulty and they were forced to live in an environment and energy of lack.

They were never given proper books, had very limited and basic food. If there clothes or the bed linen in their house were torn, the father refused to get them new clothes and they had to make do with mending and repairing those same torn clothes.

This established an unhealthy relationship with money right from childhood and impacted my client even in his adulthood despite he himself being okay with and having enough money and not being miserly with it. He just couldn't believe that the money would keep flowing and he didn't feel safe with it.

So I addressed and healed his childhood trauma with multi modality healings such as hypnosis, inner-child healing, **money reiki** and regual reiki at the deepest level, peeling off one layer after another.

The client himself learnt reiki and money reiki so he could continue working on himself. The entire process did take time and patience, but today after 6 months of healing work, finally, he has a settled and happy relationship with money and feels safe and aligned with money energy.

Why don't Prosperity Teachings, Positive Affirmations and the Law of Attraction work for you?

Now at this point, many of you may be thinking that, hey, we know this.

We know that our energy is what is stopping us from attracting, receiving and retaining wealth and a steady flow of money.

That is why we are working with prosperity teachings, doing positive affirmations and visualizing abundance, wealth and money.

We have done it all, worked with the best prosperity mentors, and invested money consistently in healing sessions and abundance/prosperity courses, and yet here we are still struggling with our relationship with money.

Why does nothing seem to work for us???

There's Good News Yet!

I understand your confusion and your frustration. I have at least a couple of clients every day who are dealing with such serious issues with money, and it keeps running away from them. But I have good news yet!

Irrespective of your current relationship with money, the good news is that it is **possible to completely clear your existing negative and limiting energy with regard to money and reboot your relationship with it.**

While having said that, it's completely possible to reboot your energetic relationship with money, I have a rider to add on top of that. Don't expect miracles to happen immediately. Be patient, seek proper guidance and healing and do the work required to clear your energy as guided by a trained and expert healer.

Why? You may ask? Well, because before any of these things can begin to work for you and before you begin to attract and retain wealth and money, you must be in alignment with the energy of money!

And if you are struggling with money, it is clear that you aren't in alignment with its energy. Therefore it is time to clear and unblock your money energy.

The Multiple Levels of Money Energy

However, it is at this level that most teachers, experts, and practitioners make the mistake of not being able to clear their money energy at the grassroots level because they do not understand the existence of money energy at various levels.

Money energy though very pure and positive at the spiritual level, can be very complex and chaotic in its physical form in our world.

It is important for you to understand that your money energy impacts you at 3 major levels.

- The Universal Level
- The Ancestral Level
- The Individual Level

In the section below, I have explained these levels with examples. And **unless you clear and unblock this energy at all these levels, you will never be aligned with the manifesting energy of money** where you can receive and grow your money and wealth consistently.

Here's the Hitch- The Universal Money Energy

Now most healers, prosperity teachers and success experts tell you **that money is only a tool and a means of exchange, that it is neither good nor bad and embodies neutral energy.** So you should not shy away from or feel bad and guilty about amassing wealth and creating/attracting money.

In theory, that sounds great, it seems logical, too, and you start to work on changing your energy. You say affirmations like: I am a money magnet; I welcome money from varied sources. Then you sit and even visualize yourself receiving that wealth and spending it. And you keep expecting miracles to happen and big sums of money to flow into your life.

While you are doing this, you are seeing money being spent on warfare and nuclear weapons and on training terrorists. You see images of people dying of hunger in Africa and other poor areas. You see slum dwellers in your own country and despite all your prosperity. **It is difficult for your subconscious to believe that money is neutral energy, and without even realizing it, you subconsciously begin repelling it.**

This is the universal energy of money, and it is directly affecting your energetic relationship with money.

Lineage to Lineage a Pattern is built, and a Block created- The Ancestral Money Energy

Similarly, if most of your efforts to make money and build wealth are falling flat, it is possible that there could be a pattern of blocked money energy patterns that have been solidified through various generations.

For example, maybe your ancestors faced famine and ended up having to live frugally. Thus this energy of fear and lack got passed down through generations, making you believe that you deserve to live an austere and hard life without luxuries. **This ancestral blockage of wealth energy could be the reason you end up repelling money.**

So long as this energetic pattern keeps being passed on, all the people in your family will find it challenging to allow money to stay in their lives and build a stable relationship with it.

Now you might wonder, at this point, how can I possibly know what the roots of my ancestral blockages are? Next, you might be terrified that you might never be able to clear these ancestral patterns since you are incapable of identifying them.

Relax, don't worry. To clear your ancestral blockages, it isn't necessary for either you or the healer/energy expert guiding you to know the specifics of your patterns. It can be done completely and successfully with intention, and the only critical factor is the expertise and experience of the healer involved.

What Kind of Money Energy do you give out? The Individual Money Energy

Even if your world view of money energy is neutral and you are also fortunate enough to have no negative ancestral patterns regarding money in your lineage, you could still end up repelling money unconsciously.

This could be because your individual energy regarding money does not flow clearly. These could be general blocks and imbalances in your life due to any negative circumstances or trauma you might be going through, such as a severe illness, a toxic environment or an abusive relationship. Or they could be specific beliefs about money.

For example, as a child, you may have seen on the news a very rich man being sent to jail because he had built his empire on fraud and unethical practices. **Now, this might cause you to develop the subconscious belief that money can only be earned through unethical means, and you being an ethical person, may keep repelling it.**

As we have already discussed, if your energy and aura are blocked, it will be impossible to attract anything good in your life, including money.

Prepare the Field for a Great Harvest: Clear & Heal

Just as you need to prepare the field well before sowing the seeds in order to receive a bumper harvest.

Similarly, if you want to manifest money and wealth in a consistent, trusted and guaranteed manner. You have to ensure you prepare your energy field and energy system first.

You need to remove weeds and make the soil fertile before sowing the seeds, and then you need to nurture and water them carefully to receive your bumper harvest.

Similarly, you need to clear the weeds of unwanted money blocks and patterns, then have a clear, free-flowing and open energy field to be in alignment with the energy of money.

This energy clearing can be performed through many energy healing modalities. What I majorly use in conjunction with other modalities as per the need is the powerful Money Reiki clearing & healing technique.

This technique clears your energy and beliefs right from the root at all three levels, universal, ancestral and personal. And then onwards gives you guidelines and rituals to sustain this clearing and build Money Reiki into your way of life for continued results.

Once you've cleared your money & wealth energy at all these levels, you can begin using all your prosperity rituals and affirmations to attract money, and they will soon begin to make a difference.

Warning Words of Caution!

Even when you understand the secret and powerful concept of clearing your energy at the 3 different levels, remember not to compare your results with anyone else because each person's energy systems, levels of blockage and the stubbornness of patterns will be different from one another's.

The time taken to clear and heal will vary for everyone. However, what is guaranteed is that it is definitely possible under the guidance of an expert and experienced master energy healer.

Also, you must remember that energy imbalances, blockages and ancestral patterns can be quite stubborn and deep-rooted. Clearing them from the root takes a lot of patience and time. You may encounter one layer after another. Whenever you feel you have hit a plateau in your manifestation, you can be sure that your energy is blocked and there is something that needs to be cleared. Therefore be patient, keep peeling off and clearing the layers step by gentle step with your healer.

Practical Guidance

Here are some simple yet powerful steps that you can take to begin clearing your energy right away:

- Set the intention that you are clearing any blockages at the personal, ancestral and universal levels that are causing you to repel money.

- Choose a symbol that you associate with money, it could be anything that speaks of money and wealth to you. It could be the popular Dollar symbol $ also.

- Visualize this symbol coming out of the palms of your hands several times during the day or whenever you want to. See it floating around you joyfully in your auric field.

- Always bless your money when you spend it, thanking it for the good it has done you and for the good it will do to whoever receives it.

- Create a money and wealth energy box. Choose a box, clean and decorate it with symbols of money and any other pictures of wealth and abundance goals you may have.

- Write down up to 3 money goals. Write them in the present tense, for example

- I make Rs. 50000/month.

- I manage my money wisely and efficiently.

- I have enough money to buy a 3 bedroom home.

- Add any pictures, objects, or newspaper clippings that will add to your intention. Then place your hands on the box with intention and send energy to it, visualizing the symbol you had chosen earlier and bless the box.

And here, as a special gift, is the link to my Global Money Healing Guided Meditation, which is extremely powerful and I use effectively with my clients to clear money energy at the universal level.

Chapter 8

UNBLOCK Your HEALTH:
[Physical, Mental & Spiritual]

"You could stand here sick with 10 illnesses today, and tomorrow have no evidence of any of them."

~Anonymous

So, the above statement in the box might sound shocking and rather radical to you, and it is indeed, BUT IT IS ALSO TRUE.

From the previous chapters, it becomes very clear to us that everything within and around us is the way it is because of our thought patterns and our vibrations.

So is the case with disease. Your body is the first thing that responds to your vibration. So any and all dis-ease or distress in your body is so because of your own feelings, emotions, thoughts and energy.

And obviously, if your thoughts are what has created this reality of disease, **then you are certainly capable of changing your thought and energy to replace disease with health because the Universe totally supports you in every thought you choose to think and believe.**

The Four Emotional Foundations of Diseases

As the great Louise Hay in her "heal your body philosophy and system" says, Resentment, Fear, Guilt and Criticism are the 4 emotions that are the cause of all baggage and disease in your body.

These emotions don't just stay as emotions; they manifest as physical symptoms of disease in your body as they block your Aura and energy.

In order to do away with these emotions, you need to stop blaming people and take ownership and responsibility for your own life. You cannot stop people from behaving poorly, but that does not mean you have to be affected by it or react to it. You must not let people's opinions affect your energy. As this gives rise to disease.

Constant resentment due to not being able to do, say or live as you want can lead to Cancer in your body.

Criticism from others and, more importantly, from yourselves will result in Arthritis in the body.

Guilt is another killing emotion; when you feel guilty, you feel you have done something wrong and deserve to be punished for it. You serve this punishment to your body in the form of pain.

Finally, fear can be of various types, of the future, of the unknown, of success, failure, rejection etc., and fear causes tension. This tension can physically manifest as baldness, ulcers, sore feet etc.

Forgiveness: The Masterkey to Health

Whatever the Source of disease or blockage in your energy system, there is only one master cure for all ailments; FORGIVENESS for the self and others.

So here's my simple advice to you, the moment you are ill or sick, ask yourself who or what it is that you need to forgive. It could be a situation, another person(s) or yourself.

Here's another thumb rule to live by in such a situation, whoever or whatever you find the hardest to forgive is what is causing you the most distress and holding the disease in your body.

A state of unforgiveness is an open invitation to sickness. You must forgive yourself and others for all that happened in the past, all the hurts, resentments, regrets and guilts; they serve you no longer. They only keep you locked in sickness and disease.

Based on Louise Hay's system and what I practice, I am sharing with you the most common thought patterns related to your major body parts that lead to most diseases and how you can overcome them.

Please note that not every cause will apply 100 % to everyone. However, it will be at least 90-95 % of the reason behind the disease.

Body Parts-Thought Patterns-Disease

- Let's begin from the top of **the body with the HEAD.** The head symbolizes us, and it is a representation of us as a whole. Consequently, something being wrong in the head area means we believe something is wrong with us, and we do not like or love ourselves as a whole. In such a situation, we must begin to forgive and love ourselves. Headaches mean you think you are wrong; delve deep and see where you think you are wrong and forgive yourself. Migraines are created by the desire and pressure to be perfect and the anger at not being so. Forgive yourself for not being perfect. Release the anger and love yourself to health.

- Then comes our **HAIR- it symbolizes our strength;** however, when we feel tense or afraid, our tension begins in our shoulders and comes up to our scalp. This results in balding and other hair concerns. Here we must practice grounding, centering and relaxation. Even consciously asking our scalp to relax will begin to make a difference.

- **The EARS, as it is obvious, are our medium of hearing.** When we face problems with our ears, it usually means that there is something we want to avoid hearing or we do not like something we are hearing or have heard. It could be criticism or conflict of any sort. Here we must take the criticism constructively and impersonally, use it if we can, ignore it if we can't and move on. If it is a conflict involving us, we must try to resolve it through talking or forgiveness. If it doesn't involve us, we must acknowledge that we are not responsible for others' behaviour and move on. Deafness, if not genetic, can imply a desire to block out conversation from those closest and the above techniques will help.

- **The EYES, as it is obvious, are our medium of seeing.** When we face problems with our eyes, it usually means that there is something we want to avoid seeing or we do not like something we are seeing or have seen. It could be something about ourselves or our life. It could be either in the past or the present, or even the way we think our life is shaping up in the future. When we find ourselves unable to control or change our experience, we try and shut our eyes to it. If you go back in time a little before your eye problems began and search for an event that you wanted to block out and resolve it through forgiveness or love, you will find your eyes healing.

- **SINUS problems in the face & nose area are** a sure sign that we are irritated by someone close to us. Here we need to remind ourselves that we are responsible for our own power and our actions. We must stand firm in our truth and not let their actions affect us.

- Then come the NECK represents our ability to be **flexible in our life and thinking.** When we face issues with our necks, it means we are being rigid about something and not seeing the other person's point of view. In such a situation, we must remind ourselves that there is no one right way of doing things. That our way is not the only way.

- **The THROAT represents our ability to express ourselves, ask for what we want and speak our truth. It also represents our creativity.** When we have issues with our throat, for example, when we are angry about being unable to express ourselves, it could lead to sore throat or Laryngitis. Tonsilitis & Thyroid problems are manifestations of blocked or stifled creativity. The throat also symbolizes our response to change. A cough can mean resistance to change.

- Our **ARMS are our means of embracing life and its experiences.** The upper part of our arms symbolizes our capacity to embrace experiences, and the lower part our ability to do so. So when we face health issues in our arms, it means we are unable to accept and embrace our life experiences, and we need to accept the reality of our situation. Our joints store our emotions and baggage from the past and can become inflexible and painful unless we resolve these. Our elbows represent our ability to change direction in our life. If you don't let go of old emotions, you will not be able to move on in life.

- **The HANDS are our ability to clasp and grasp.** Sometimes we grasp too tightly out of fear. This leads to problems in the hands. What you need to do is relax and know that what is yours cannot be taken away from you. Each FINGER also represents where and what you need to work on. The thumb having issues means you are worrying about something. A problem in your index finger means anger and fear stemming from your ego, so you need to work on your ego. The middle finger denotes sex and anger. It could imply sexual frustration and anger. Holding the middle finger of your left hand will help you release anger at a woman and of the right hand at a man. The ring finger denotes unions and also grief. A problem here indicates problems in union or holding grief from a situation. Problems with the little finger mean you are facing family problems, or you are pretending to be something you are not and are not being your authentic self.

- If having problems with our **BACK, it means that we are feeling** unsupported, like we have to do it all alone. Here we need to remind ourselves that irrespective of how unsupported we may feel, the truth is that the Universe always has our back and is supporting us unconditionally. Problems in the upper back signify a lack of emotional support from family, friends, colleagues etc., so talk it out with them, forgive and love. Middle back problems mean you are holding guilt, so forgive yourself, and lower back problems mean fear or worry about lack of money or messy finances. So set them in order and know and affirm that you deserve abundance and you will always be provided for.

- **Our LEGS are what move us forward.** We face problems in our legs when we refuse to move forward, generally due to fear or in a specific direction. Our THIGHS become fat swollen, and painful due to stored resentment.

- Our **KNEES, like our neck, have to do with flexibility.** When we hold pride and ego and refuse t bend despite it being the right thing to do, we face problems with our knees.

- Our **FEET represent our understanding of life and our destination, and ourselves.** That is why little children prance around happily because they have so much to look forward to, and old people shuffle and drag their feet because they have little to look forward to. We must infuse ourselves with a sense of purpose and have something to look forward to keep our feet healthy.

- The **LUNGS represent our ability to take in and give out life fully.** Problems with the lungs mean an inability to live life fully. This means a fear of enjoying life. Traditionally women have been shallow breathers because they feel restricted and feel they do not deserve to enjoy life fully.

- A **problem with our BREASTS usually signifies that we are over-mothering a person, place, thing or situation** and it's time to let go and let them or it grow and evolve organically on its own. In the case of Cancer, it signifies deep-rooted resentment.

- The **HEART, of course, denotes LOVE & our BLOOD symbolizes JOY.** A heart lovingly pumping blood spreads joy throughout our body. When we feel unlovable and deny ourselves joy, that is when we suffer from angina, anemia, heart attack and other related problems.

- Our **STOMACH is responsible for digesting and assimilating all the new ideas and experiences that we come** across in life. So if you have stomach problems, then you need to stop and assess what or who it is that you are unable to stomach or digest. ULCERS happen when we believe ourselves not good enough.

- Our **GENITALS represent our core masculinity or femininity.** We face issues and concerns here when either we are not comfortable being a man or a woman, or we view our genitals, their functions and their desires as sinful or dirty. The myths and beliefs around sex, sensuality and pleasure often foster guilt in us, and this leads to genital sickness. Problems such as Vaginitis, bladder, prostate, penis and anal problems also have their origin in such beliefs. Releasing taboos around sex and pleasure goes a long way in maintaining genital health.

- **Our SKIN is our unique signature; it represents our individuality.** When we suffer from skin diseases, it signifies that our individuality is being stifled, and we feel powerless and judged not enough by others. A speedy way to overcome skin problems is to affirm to yourself wholeheartedly, multiple times a day, "I approve of myself!"

- **ACCIDENTS are no accidents; we create and invite them subconsciously.** We create them to express anger and serve ourselves punishment. The area and degree of the accident will tell you what area you want to punish yourself in and how much.

Delving into the Disease

Now let's quickly look at common categories of diseases and their root causes.

- **Anorexia-Bulimia is an eating disorder that stems from a hatred of the self.** Denying yourself food means denying yourself life. However, hatred is only a thought pattern that needs to be replaced with self-love.

- **Arthritis is a result of constant criticism,** of the self, of others and of the self from others. This is resolved through letting go of perfectionism and loving self and others, and accepting the self and others As-Is.

- **Asthma occurs due to smothering,** people who suffer from over protection, over care and over instruction, so they feel they can't breathe. They feel guilty and not good enough.

- **Boils, Burns, Cuts, Fever, Sores etc, are all expressions of anger in the body.** It is, therefore important to express your anger and truth in words rather than bottling it up yourself.

- **Cancer, as I have already mentioned, is the manifestation of long and deep resentment that eats away at the body literally.** It could be the result of a childhood event even. It can only be dissolved through deep, unconditional and ongoing forgiveness of the self and others.

- **Obesity or being overweight stems from a need for self-protection** through physical layers of fat to avoid the hurts caused due to criticism, rejection, betrayal, insults etc., either perceived or real. It can be dissolved through approving and loving yourself and trusting in the process of life.

- **Pain in any form or in any part of the body is a punishment for guilt** and can be resolved through forgiveness.

- **Strokes are blood clots formed due to a lack of joy due to negative** thinking. Shifting energy through positive thought patterns and actions and believing yourself worthy of joy will prevent strokes.

- **Stiffness in the body definitely means rigidity in mind.** What old patterns do you need to shed to move forward?

- **Swelling in the body means you are clinging to old hurts and unexpressed tears.** It implies you are feeling trapped. You need to resolve this through forgiveness and letting go.

- **Tumors are false growths due to nursing old hurts and unworthiness.** Here you need to remind yourself that just because certain jobs or relationships failed doesn't mean you are unworthy.

With all the information I have shared with you until now, especially in this chapter, you surely understand that your health and well-being are primarily your own creation and within your control.

The two most critical keys to unlocking and maintaining health are self-love and forgiveness. With these two powerful tools, it is possible to dissolve even the most deep-rooted cause of disease.

The Astrology, Numerology & Vaastu of Health

While thought and energy are the primary causes of health or disease in a person, as a multi-modality healer, I can tell you that there are certain other factors too that have a powerful impact on your health.

These are factors such as the **Astrological placement of planets in your natal chart.** In addition to your energy and thought patterns, the way your planets are aligned in your astrological chart will affect your health. Certain placements bode ill for your health; however, the effects of such placements can be remedied or mitigated with the help and guidance of an experienced astrologer. Therefore whenever facing health issues, it would be beneficial to have your astrological chart reviewed.

Numerology also impacts your health powerfully. If there are certain significant numbers missing in your numerological grid, it could be an indicator of ill health. If your name does not numerologically match your psychic number, then too your health and well-being can be disrupted. Also, if your psychic number or destiny number is not in sync with your life path number, it will lead to breakdowns in health. Additionally, certain people have some karmic numbers in their numerological chart; these karmic numbers impact a person's health powerfully. Therefore it is essential to have your numerological chart reviewed by an experienced numerologist and then follow their guidance to overcome health challenges.

Health issues can also be the result of wrong Vaastu placements in your home or place of work. For example, if the toilet seat is in the east, where ideally we place Gods & Godesses, then the residents are likely to face major health issues as the ancestral (Pittra) energies would be disturbed. All their money would be spent on battling and treating these health issues.

If someone keeps having recurring health issues, it signifies that the east of their home is malefic, and this needs to be immediately remedied.

If the southwest direction of any house has underground sewers, then the lady of the house can suffer from digestive tract issues.

If the north of a home has heavy almirahs or objects, the residents will suffer from headaches, especially migraines.

If the center of the house, the Brahmasthan, has heavy objects, the chances of diseases like cancer become very high.

These are just a few examples. There are many more such Vaastu doshas that could lead to health challenges.

Therefore when facing health challenges, you must focus on your thought and energy first, but you must not overlook the importance of an all-round approach to addressing your health problems.

Chapter 9

UNBLOCK Your RELATIONSHIPS

*"Blame keeps wounds open. Forgiveness
and Self-Love are the healers."*

~Anonymous

Life is a Roller-Coaster of Relationships

Your life revolves around relationships. You have a relationship with literally everything. And this does not just include people, and other living beings, you have relationships with places and inanimate objects too.

It has already been established in earlier chapters that you have energetic relationships with everything and are interconnected through vibration. In fact you even have a relationship with what you are reading right now.

So basically your relationships are a constant exchange or flow of energy between you and the person/place/object of the relationship.

All your relationships however are driven by one single thing only and that is your relationship with yourself.

You are Your You Universe

And **the relationship you have with yourself is shaped and defined by the relationship you had with the adults around you when you were a child.**

As a child interacting with the adults round you, your parents, relatives, neighbors, teachers etc. and the environment around you, **you develop beliefs based on what you experience.**

Most of the time these beliefs are not universal truths, they do not apply to all situations and neither are they facts. **They are just the experiences you happened to have. More often than not these beliefs are limiting and damaging to your relationships.**

For example if you had an abusive parent that is just your experience it does not mean that all parents are abusive. But your belief might affect your relationship with your children. You may either believe being abusive is the only way to parent or you may want to avoid being like your parent and may over compensate and pamper your children silly or you could end up being a balanced parent avoiding emulating the behaviour of your toxic parent without over compensating.

Or as a child, if you were constantly told that you were useless, unlovable and couldn't do anything right then you might carry those insecurities into your relationships and you may feel unloved for no reason making you feel dissatisfied with the relationship.

In a nut shell please understand that it is your inner child and the beliefs that it holds from childhood which is impacting all your relationships.

Relationships are Fragile: Handle with Care

Relationships have always been delicate but nowadays they have become even more so. Today relationships are fraught with anxiety, discontent, resentment, infidelity and breakups at the drop of a hat.

Ups and downs are normal in life and relationships, regrettably today there are more downs than ups in most relationships. All relationships, be they in your personal life or at work, are becoming short-lived and are ready to explode as everyone is on a short fuse these days.

All these changes are a reflection of our environment, where stress and ego have taken center stage. There are many reasons why you are not able to sustain relationships, but the solution is pretty much universal.

The first step to balancing and harmonizing a relationship is becoming aware that there is a concern in the relationship.

This is fundamental because if you do not see a problem, you will never acknowledge it leave alone to address and resolve it.

To change or heal the situation, you need to first introspect rather than just blaming the other person in the relationship and expecting them to change according to us. You need to see and discover what is blocking us from having a harmonious relationship, what is the behaviour, belief or expectation that you can change to have the desired results.

You must try and identify f there is a pattern buried deep in your actions. Is it the objective truth, or is it a limiting belief you formed as a child?

Once you've identified the blockage or pattern, you must evaluate your belief system. Is what you perceive the truth, or is it merely an assumption basis your limiting beliefs?

To resolve differences in relationships, it is essential not to play the blame game. Do not keep making excuses like "I'm unlucky in relationships", "God never favors me", "the Universe does not support me etc.". Take responsibility for your own happiness and take action to change what needs to be changed. At the end of the chapter, I will be sharing remedies and Upayas to take action and work on your own self and thus your relationships.

Forgiveness & Self-Love: The Keys to the Kingdom

As I shared earlier, the self-worth issues that you form as a child impact your relationships. You project your perceived unworthiness and insecurities onto your relationships. You say things like, "It's all my fault." "I am too dumb to understand my partner". "I can do nothing right; no wonder they don't love me." I am not good enough for them.".

The key is to accept that these are your limiting beliefs and patterns. Many times people stay in denial and do not take responsibility for their actions or lack of them. Acknowledgement and acceptance are the keys to healing your relationship with yourself and, consequently, others.

To acknowledge and accept your patterns, it is essential that you first forgive yourself for all that you blame yourself for. Forgiveness will clear your blockages and patterns. Forgive yourself for known and unknown mistakes, for you were only doing your best under the circumstances as you knew then.

After you forgive yourself, forgive all others who have wronged you or not come up to expectations, in truth or perception. Also, ask for forgiveness in your own mind or personally from those who you feel you may have wronged.

Forgive, forgive and ask to be forgiven. That is the surest and fastest way of clearing energy blockages in relationships. However, remember that all forgiveness has to begin with yourself.

Once we forgive ourselves and accept ourselves just as we are, that is true self-love, and when we love ourselves and are secure about our worth, that is when we become secure in our relationships.

The Spiritual Dimension of Relationships
Soulmates, Twinflames, Soul Family and Family Constellations

The physical manifestation of relationships in this material world is a reflection of our relationships carried from our spiritual/soul plane. There is generally a group of souls that begins its journey together from the spiritual dimension and continues to traverse through lifetimes together as a soul group.

This group of people keeps reincarnating in different relationships with each other, evolving and growing while learning and teaching lessons to one another. In one lifetime, they could be parents and children; in another, spouses or siblings or close friends and colleagues in yet another one.

These people are our soul family, our soul mates. A soul mate is not necessarily a romantic partner only. They may come to us in any relationship, and their purpose is to help us evolve and learn the lessons that we have chosen as our purpose for coming to Earth.

In one lifetime, the same person may teach us painful lessons, while in another lifetime, they could be in the most loving bond with us.

The purpose of relationships from a spiritual perspective is also forgiveness and unconditional love. Challenging relationships are also a means to our purpose. They help us learn patience and forgiveness and assist us in developing strength of character.

So when you face issues in marriage or relationships, they are being carried over not just from your childhood but from previous lifetimes even. Get to the root of these causes, learn the lessons, heal the hurts and then move forward.

However, this brings us to one of the most burning questions, does this mean we should continue to stay in toxic relationships? Is a divorce or walking out of toxic relationships wrong?

NO! The answer is a BIG NO.

After we have given it our best and still see no change in the relationship for the better, we owe it to ourselves to walk out of that relationship before it drains us completely. In such cases, separation or divorce is not wrong; that is the lesson-choosing yourself, learning when to say no and loving and respecting yourself enough to walk away. That is the divine purpose of that relationship.

Since you are the center of your relationships, it is necessary to heal your inner child and heal your generational and ancestral relationship patterns to resolve your relationship concerns. Also, as shared earlier, your astrological and numerological chart, along with Vastu positions in your home, will play a significant role in your relationships.

A trained, sincere and experienced healer can successfully lead you through navigating all your relationship troubles smoothly and safely.

MASTER Your ENERGY-Master YOUR Life!

BONUS REMEDIES!

So dear readers, now that you understand the importance of energy and the ways to clear, unblock and master it and activate the law of attraction, you are all geared up for a great life.

To kick-start your divine journey to mastering your energy and, thus, your life as promised, I am sharing with you my wonderfully effective remedies to bring your energy and life into balance so that you can have all that you desire and deserve.

Follow and practice these with belief and consistency, and you will see your life bloom into prosperity in every area.

Remedies for Health

1. To promote GREAT HEALTH, you must light a candle or lamp in the North-East direction of your home.

Remedies for Business, Career & Wealth

1. To improve your career & business, donate rice to the underprivileged on Ekadashi (the 11th day of the monthly lunar cycle).

2. To improve relationships in career and business, put green vegetables into a well and pray to Lord Ganesha at your workplace on Wednesdays.

3. To improve relationships in career and business, don't waste salt and water as it affects your Sun & Moon.

4. To improve relationships in career and business, feed curd and rice to crows as crows are the vehicle of Shani (Saturn), and Saturn has a positive affect on your profession.

5. To improve relationships in career and business, keep paath of Sunderkand at regular intervals. This is especially effective for businesses run by joint families.

Remedies for Love & Marriage

1. To win over your love, offer a flute at a Krishna Temple near your home.

2. To be married to your love, in a small silver bowl, mix cow's milk, shakkar (unrefined sugar), and cooked white rice. On Chaturthi (the 4th day of the monthly lunar cycle) at the time of moonrise, offer this mixture to the moon while visualizing your partner's face in the moon.

3. If marriage discussions fail in the last stages repeatedly, practice removing your footwear before entering the room.

4. On the first Thursday of the waxing moon, take 2 coins, one a silver coin and the other a rupee coin. Offer them to a Peepal tree. Bury these coins near the Peepal tree. Leave the tool used for digging near the tree only and pray for a smooth marriage.

5. To be married to your love, make rotis with turmeric added to the dough early morning on Thursdays. Keep gud (jaggery) on them and feed them to a cow. While feeding the cow, whisper your partner's name in the cow's ears. Do this for 7 consecutive Thursdays and see the effect.

6. To be married to your love, boil 8 Chhuare (dried dates) in water on a Friday night. Keep these dates along with the water at the head of your bed while sleeping. On Saturday morning, after taking a bath, release the dates and water into any flowing water source near you. Think of your desired partner while doing so.

7. To be married to your love, fast on Tuesdays. Pray at a Devi Temple and offer the Goddess red roses. Write your partner's name on a slip of paper and hide it between the flowers you offer.

Remedies for Relationships

1. Chanting "Om Lakshmi Narayan Namah" 3 times a day for 3 months will bring emotional stability to your relationship as it will bring you closer to your partner.

2. To enhance love in a relationship, light a Deepak (earthen lamp) in the South-West corner of your home. Add Nagkesar to the oil and 2 cloves to the Deepak.

3. For a great marital relationship, the master bedroom should be placed in the South-West direction and never in the North-East, especially when a woman is pregnant, to avoid miscarriage and complications.

Remedies for Black Magic

1. To reduce the effects of Black Magic, take a black thread and tie seven knots on it at equal distances. Rotate seven dried red chillies over the thread seven times and wrap them in a black cloth. Burn the cloth outside your home/building, putting some oil on it. Then wear the black thread on your right ankle.

2. To reduce the effects of Black Magic, take black Rai (mustard), Tulsi leaves, Mint leaves, Lemon peel, til (sesame seeds), and Nilgiri oil/leaves and boil all this in water for 7 minutes and divide it into seven portions. Separately pour each portion over your body. Do this consecutively for seven days.

Special Energy Tip

1. Burning Camphor in various parts of the house is very effective in neutralizing negative energy.